Cool STEAM Careers

Petroleum Engineer

Wil Mara

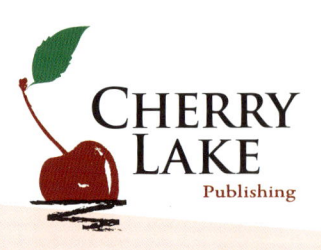

Published in the United States of America by Cherry Lake Publishing
Ann Arbor, Michigan
www.cherrylakepublishing.com

Content Adviser: Alfred William Eustes III, Ph.D., P.E., Colorado School of Mines, Petroleum Engineering Department, Golden, Colorado
Reading Adviser: Marla Conn, ReadAbility, Inc.

Photo Credits: ©branislavpudar/Shutterstock Images, cover, 1, 19; ©Lisa F. Young/Shutterstock Images, 5; ©Enjoylife/CanStockPhoto, 7; ©Alfred William Eustes III, 8, 16, 23, 24; ©Monkey Business Images/Shutterstock Images, 11; ©michaeljung/Shutterstock Images, 12; ©auremar/Shutterstock Images, 15; ©Danny E Hooks/Shutterstock Images, 21; ©alexjey/Shutterstock Images, 27; ©cozyta/Shutterstock Images, 28

Copyright ©2015 by Cherry Lake Publishing
All rights reserved. No part of this book may be reproduced or utilized in
any form or by any means without written permission from the publisher.

Library of Congress Cataloging-in-Publication Data

Mara, Wil.
 Petroleum engineer / Wil Mara.
     pages cm. — (Cool STEAM careers)
 Summary: "Readers will learn what it takes to succeed as a petroleum engineer. The book also explains the necessary educational steps, useful character traits, and daily job tasks related to this career, in the framework of the STEAM (Science, Technology, Engineering, Art, and Math) movement. Photos, a glossary, and additional resources are included."—Provided by publisher.
 Audience: Ages 8-12
 Grades: 4 to 6
 Includes index.
 ISBN 978-1-63362-005-6 (hardcover) — ISBN 978-1-63362-083-4 (pdf) — ISBN 978-1-63362-044-5 (pbk.) — ISBN 978-1-63362-122-0 (ebook) 1. Petroleum engineers—Juvenile literature. 2. Petroleum engineering—Juvenile literature. I. Title.

TN870.3.M37 2015
665.5023—dc23
                                          2014031777

Cherry Lake Publishing would like to acknowledge the work of
The Partnership for 21st Century Skills. Please visit *www.p21.org*
for more information.

Printed in the United States of America
Corporate Graphics

ABOUT THE AUTHOR

Wil Mara is an award-winning and best-selling author of more than 150 books, many of which are educational titles for young readers. Further information about his work can be found at www.wilmara.com.

TABLE OF CONTENTS

CHAPTER 1
Liquid Gold 4

CHAPTER 2
What It Takes 10

CHAPTER 3
Day to Day 14

CHAPTER 4
Ups and Downs 20

CHAPTER 5
Looking Ahead 26

THINK ABOUT IT 30
LEARN MORE 31
GLOSSARY 32
INDEX 32

STEAM is the acronym for Science, Technology, Engineering, Arts, and Mathematics. In this book, you will read about how each of these study areas is connected to a career in petroleum engineering.

— CHAPTER 1 —

Liquid Gold

Jessica helped her mom fill up their car's tank when they stopped at a gas station. She was sure the gasoline was stored in great quantity underground. And she figured that the pump drew the gasoline out of that storage area. "But," she asked her mother, "is it someone's job to design how the gasoline is stored and then transferred into cars?"

"Definitely," her mom said. "It all starts with a **petroleum** engineer."

Petroleum is one of the most useful and abundant

substances in the world. Known as a **fossil fuel**, petroleum is found deep in the earth. It comes from the slow decay of organisms that died long ago, and whose remains have been subject to great pressure and heat.

Gasoline that comes from a gas pump is stored in large tanks under the ground.

Petroleum exists in liquid or gas form, and its color ranges from a beautiful honey yellow to a thick, inky black. Thousands of products are made from it. When the price goes up for this "liquid gold," as some call it, there is a ripple effect throughout the global economy. When the price goes down, just about everybody breathes easier. The world uses about 100 million **barrels** per day, so without it, life would be very different.

For many centuries, petroleum has been used for lighting, heating, food preparation, and medicine. But until fairly recently, nations didn't see it as a basis for war, and it didn't have a huge effect on the world's economy. All that changed in the mid-19th century.

In 1847, Scottish chemist James Young figured out a way to **distill** petroleum to produce a form of oil that could be burned in lamps. The demand for this product grew very quickly. But after a few years, Young ran into a problem—the oil supply he was tapping, which came from a local coal mine, ran out, and he was

Oil tankers like this one transport oil around the world.

forced to seek another source. Sensing tremendous business opportunities, others soon began seeking claims on their own oil **deposits**.

The first well drilled specifically for oil was completed in Titusville, Pennsylvania. It was 69.5 feet (21 meters) deep. This well produced 20 barrels of oil a day. In the United States in 1859, only about 2,000 barrels of petroleum were drawn out of the ground. Just 10 years later, that number skyrocketed to more than four million.

Today, with the global demand for petroleum at mind-boggling levels, there is an equal demand for workers who

This is the Drake Well, built in Titusville, Pennsylvania more than 150 years ago.

understand the complicated science and art of petroleum **extraction**. The good news for anyone thinking about a career in petroleum engineering is that the work, while not always easy, is interesting, will take you to many places around the world, and pays quite well.

THINK ABOUT SCIENCE

Geology is one of the most important sciences, because a petroleum engineer must figure out how to drill through the earth's surface to get to what's beneath it. Physics is important as it deals with matter, force, motion, and energy. Chemistry is also critical because a variety of chemicals are used to aid in the removal of petroleum once deposits are found.

What It Takes

Say a company finds a rich deposit of petroleum somewhere but doesn't know the most efficient way to get it out of the ground and into pipelines and tanks. That's when a company turns to a petroleum engineer: the problem solver.

A petroleum engineer (PE) is an educated person. At the very least, a professional PE will have a bachelor's degree (a four-year degree), although fewer than 20 colleges offer accredited degree programs specifically in petroleum engineering. However, bachelor's

After you've earned a degree, you will receive additional hands-on training in an entry-level position.

degrees are offered in mechanical engineering and chemical engineering, both of which are useful. As for math, learning algebra, trigonometry, and calculus is required, while for science, you would take physics, chemistry, **thermodynamics**, and others. You may want to earn a postgraduate degree, such as a master's or a doctorate. With these studies you will gain advanced knowledge in everything from geology to thermodynamics.

Once you've obtained your degree and have been

Petroleum engineers often work at the job site.

hired for an entry-level position, your employer may very well give you further training in petroleum engineering. Each company helps its employees develop skills that it values. You will likely be working in an office and very often in the field as well. Your job may even become a kind of apprenticeship, where you are learning while working. In these instances, you will likely have an experienced petroleum engineer as a mentor.

Perhaps the most important quality you'll need is **analytical** skills. As a problem solver, you have to be someone who can stop and take the time to patiently study a situation in detail, so you can come up with a reasonable, workable solution that honors safety, the environment, the public, and economics.

Some personal confidence is also necessary. Remember—your employer will be depending on you for accurate information. The decisions you make may lead to massive investments in time, energy, and money.

THINK ABOUT ART

Even with all the math and science, there's still an artistic side to petroleum engineering. Every time you encounter a petroleum-extraction challenge, you will need to think "outside the box" because every situation will be a little different. It's at this point—finding that critical solution—that some creative thinking will be required.

Day to Day

A petroleum engineer's daily duties may be at the office, in a laboratory, or out in the field. Very often, engineers have to travel to the far-off locations where petroleum deposits have been discovered. An engineer might be away from home for long periods of time. If you're the type of person who enjoys travel, then this aspect of the job will be highly appealing to you. Sometimes, the engineer may be called to a drilling site on very short notice. Some engineers find themselves following a routine 40-hour workweek, while other times the hours can be twice as long.

The engineer is often the go-to person for the entire extraction project. The engineer first determines the most sensible way to extract the oil and then oversees the process to make sure it all goes smoothly. Once a petroleum deposit has been discovered, the engineer

A petroleum engineer studies many kinds of maps.

Located on Alaska's North Slope, this rig didn't drill straight down. It drills lateral, or sideways, holes thousands of feet out of a single well.

collects all the data necessary to evaluate the site. The engineer will study maps that show not only the location of the petroleum but also rock formations and **fault lines**. He or she will also consult experts in related fields, other engineers, and scientists.

Once the engineer understands the situation, he will plan an approach to extracting the oil. This is often where the biggest obstacles lie because it's not always a matter of simply drilling in a straight line and then running a pipe down there. Sometimes the engineer must take a more unconventional route, such as drilling vertically downward to a certain point and then turning in a different direction. This is known as **directional drilling**. The PE may feel it is best to design and then utilize a computer simulation beforehand. Also, the PE has to consider which **additives** might need to be fed into the deposit—such as water, steam, or chemicals—in order to draw the petroleum out of the ground more easily.

THINK ABOUT ENGINEERING

An engineer is someone who pulls together scientific and mathematical information in order to create something with practical value. In other words, an engineer takes something from the abstract (the information) to the concrete (the solution). Engineers like studying a problem and coming up with a method for solving it.

Once all the drilling and extraction equipment is in place, the petroleum engineer has to run tests to make sure all equipment is installed properly and in top working condition. This is particularly important with new equipment, especially if it is a new, customized design. This testing will ensure the protection of people and the environment. The engineer may also make sure the crew operating the equipment is fully qualified. In this regard, a PE has to be a bit of a human resources manager.

Once drilling begins, the engineer will help monitor the process. If there is an unexpected problem, he or she will be one of the first people everyone turns to for the solution. During the entire process, a PE will also be thinking about new and better ways to drill and extract in the future. Every project is a potential learning opportunity.

Petroleum engineers monitor equipment performance and find solutions if there are any problems.

[COOL STEAM CAREERS]

19

Ups and Downs

Like any other profession, being a petroleum engineer has its upsides and its downsides. It is important to learn as much as you can about both so your expectations of this career will be sensible and realistic.

Petroleum engineering itself doesn't present much in the way of danger. Your life will not be on the line on a regular basis. Still, accidents do happen sometimes at drilling sites. The infamous *Deepwater Horizon* oil spill that occurred in 2010 in the Gulf of Mexico began with an explosion on the oil rig that resulted in the death of

Drilling site accidents can result in oil spills that contaminate nearby land and water.

[COOL STEAM CAREERS]

11 workers, with many more injured. Also, petroleum engineers are sometimes required to travel to unfriendly areas where people may not be happy about foreigners drilling on their land. Depending on where the drilling and production take place, security may become an important issue.

Petroleum engineering is also a fairly competitive profession since the pay is quite good but there is a tendency for the job market to go through broad swings. There will be times when many companies are hiring and it seems as though there aren't enough engineers to fill all the positions. Then, without warning, those same jobs will vanish, and some engineers who have jobs will be laid off. The price of oil changes constantly, which affects how many positions are needed. So even if you find a job, there's no guarantee as to how long you'll be able to keep it.

On the other hand, there are some terrific benefits to being a petroleum engineer. According to the U.S.

Petroleum engineers with a lot of experience are in demand.

Traveling to a drill site is common for a petroleum engineer.

Bureau of Labor Statistics, the median annual salary of a petroleum engineer is almost $150,000. The median salary is the wage that half the workers earned more than and half earned less than. With this kind of money, you could live quite comfortably and easily save enough to retire at an earlier age than most of your peers. And in spite of the unpredictable job market, those who manage to gain enough experience and build solid reputations will always find themselves in demand.

A petroleum engineer spends a fair amount of time

in an office environment, working alone, studying reports, and poring over maps. This gives you a certain degree of freedom and **autonomy**, which most people prefer over constant supervision. No two drill sites will be the same. You will need to summon all your training and experience for each stimulating, challenging new project.

THINK ABOUT MATH

How far down should you drill? How much additive do you need to extract the petroleum? Calculations have to be made every day, and there is little room for error. This is definitely the kind of occupation where you "check your work twice, then check it again."

Looking Ahead

A good paycheck is one of the most attractive aspects of the petroleum engineering profession. Petroleum engineering is one of the few professions where a person can expect to earn a high salary with just a bachelor's degree. However, the more education you have, the higher your salary might be.

And here's some more good news. In the next 10 years, the market for petroleum engineers in the United States is expected to grow by about 25 percent, increasing from 40,000 to 50,000 jobs. Furthermore, as oil and gas extraction methods become more complex, companies will need to hire more engineers to manage the process—and more engineers may specialize in certain areas.

The job market for petroleum engineers is expected to increase in the next 10 years.

The demand for petroleum drives the building of facilities like this and provides petroleum engineers with job opportunities.

There might even be an opportunity to start your own engineering firm in the years ahead. Keeping petroleum engineers on staff can be very expensive, and more companies are instead turning to self-employed engineers. This arrangement would give you not only the benefits of running your own business, but also the freedom to work for more than one company. Those who decide to go this route should also consider basic business training in order to learn how to manage a company. Once you've developed a solid reputation and made enough contacts, you can almost be guaranteed continued employment for as long as you choose.

The demand for petroleum products continues to increase. Also, as companies become forced to find petroleum deposits in more nontraditional locations, skilled engineers who can figure out how to extract it will be in great demand. A career in petroleum engineering will continue to be very attractive.

THINK ABOUT TECHNOLOGY

In a career like petroleum engineering, better strategies and new equipment are being developed all the time. A person who keeps up on the latest technology will be the one most in demand by employers—and will have the greatest chance of success when doing the job.

THINK ABOUT IT

After reading this book, what do you think makes a petroleum engineer's job important?

Reread chapters 2 and 3. How do petroleum engineers use science and technology to perform their jobs?

Do you agree with the advantages of working for yourself as a petroleum engineer, as discussed in chapter 5?

LEARN MORE

FURTHER READING

Farndon, John. *Oil*. London; New York: DK Publishing, 2012.

Manatt, Kathleen. *Searching for Oil*. North Mankato, MN: Cherry Lake, 2008.

Spilsbury, Richard. *The Oil Industry*. New York: Rosen, 2012.

WEB SITES

Energy4me—Interview with a Petroleum Engineer
www.energy4me.org/2014/01/interview-with-a-petroleum-engineer
This is an interesting question-and-answer article with a petroleum engineer.

Energy Kids—Oil (Petroleum) Basics
www.eia.gov/KIDS/energy.cfm?page=oil_home-basics-k.cfm
Read and use the infographics to get information about oil—from how oil is formed to its effect on the environment.

Science Buddies—Petroleum Engineer
www.sciencebuddies.org/science-engineering-careers/engineering/petroleum-engineer
Find links to articles, graphs, and videos about being a petroleum engineer.

GLOSSARY

additives (AD-i-tivz) something added to a substance

analytical (an-uh-LIT-i-kuhl) able to analyze a situation and come up with a workable solution

autonomy (aw-TON-uh-mee) the quality of working independently

barrels (BAR-uhlz) standard units of measurement for crude oil, with one barrel equaling 31.5 gallons (119 liters)

deposits (dih-POZ-itz) quantities of petroleum contained in a particular space underground

directional drilling (duh-REK-shuhn-uhl DRIL-ing) drilling in a nonvertical path

distill (dih-STILL) to purify a liquid by boiling it, collecting the steam, and then letting it cool until it takes a liquid form again

extraction (ik-STRAK-shuhn) the method of removing petroleum from its underground deposit

fault lines (FAWLT LYENZ) large breaks in the earth's surface that can cause an earthquake

fossil fuel (FOS-uh FYOO-uhl) combustible material that developed from the slow decay of plants and animals

petroleum (puh-TROH-lee-uhm) a thick, oily liquid found below the earth's surface that is used to make gasoline, heating oil, and many other products

thermodynamics (thur-moh-dye-NAM-iks) the study of heat and its relation to mechanical energy

INDEX

accidents, 20–22
art, 13
drilling, 16–18, 20–22
engineering, 11, 17
math, 11, 25
oil, 6–9, 16–17, 27
petroleum, 4–6
  deposits, 14, 15–16, 29
  extraction, 9, 15, 16–18, 27
petroleum engineers
  education and training, 10–12, 26
  job prospects, 22–23, 26–29
  risks and rewards, 20–25
  salary, 9, 22, 24, 26
  skills, 12–13
  what they do, 14–19
science, 9, 11
technology, 29
travel, 9, 14, 22